MY SPORT
JUDO

Tim Wood

Photographs: Chris Fairclough

Franklin Watts

New York • London • Sydney • Toronto

23

Franklin Watts Inc
387 Park Avenue South
New York
NY 10016

Printed in Italy by G. Canale & C.S.p.A. Turin

Design: K & Co

Library of Congress Cataloguing-in-Publication Data
Wood, Tim.
   Judo / Tim Wood.
     p. cm. — (My sport)
   Summary: Outines the training, special preparation, and
techniques needed to compete successfully in judo.
   ISBN 0-531-14052-0
   1. Judo—Juvenile literature. 2. Judo—Training—Juvenile
literature. [1. Judo.] I. Title. II. Series: Wood, Tim My
sport.
   GV1114.W66 1990   89-39677
   796.8'152—dc20   CIP
                             AC

3/92

Illustrations: Angela Owen

The publishers, author and photographer would
like to thank Nicola Fairbrother, Anisah
Mohamoodally, Don Werner and the members of
Pinewood Judo Club for their help and
cooperation in the production of this book.

**A message from Nicola. The throws, holds
and armlocks shown in this book can be
dangerous and should never be used without
proper supervision. If you want to learn how
to use them properly, join a judo club.**

The judo player featured in this book is Nicola Fairbrother. She is a second dan black belt. Nicola joined a judo club at the age of eight after she and her brother had seen the sport demonstrated at an army display. Her brother gave up after two years, but Nicola carried on. She became British Schools Champion at the age of fourteen. She has won gold medals at several Open Championships and became Junior European Champion in 1987. Nicola left school in 1988 and has been training full-time since then. She is one of the top players in the country at her weight, and hopes to represent Britain in the 1992 Olympic Games.

I am a *judoka.* I train six days a week.
I start each training session with a
three mile run.

4

Back at the judo club, I work out in the gym. During part of my training I wear a special "sweat suit." Sweating helps me keep to my fighting weight of 123 pounds.

A judo player needs to be strong as well as
fit. Working with weights is an important part
6 of my training schedule.

I finish my work-out with wind sprints. It is very difficult to breathe properly during a judo fight. I train my body to cope with this by doing these eighty yard dashes while holding my breath.

More about judo

Judo techniques are divided into three main groups. These are:

1 Throwing
2 Holding
3 Armlocks and strangleholds

There are over forty-five judo throws. They are all achieved by forcing opponents off balance and then using skillfully applied leverage to throw them.

There are eight basic holds, three basic armlocks and six basic strangleholds. Contests can be won by using any of the three techniques.

8

Some judo throws

Taiotoshi
(body throw)

Ogoshi
(major hip thro

Osotogari
(major outer reaping)

Okuriashiharai
(side-sweeping
ankle throw)

Tomoenage (stomach throw)

A hold
Kesagatame (scarf hold)

An arm-lock
Udegatami (arm entanglement)

A stranglehold
Katahajime (single-wing neck lock)

The level of skill achieved by a *judoka* is shown by the color of his or her belt. Belts are awarded after special grading contests.

White   Novice
Yellow
Orange
Green
Blue
Brown
Black   Top grade

Black belts can reach higher (dan) grades. The belt remains black up to fifth dan. (Alternating red and white blocks) Sixth, seventh and eighth dans. (Red) Ninth and tenth dans.

9

Once my fitness training is finished, I put on my judo suit *(judogi)* and go into the gym *(dojo)*. I do a series of stretching exercises to loosen my joints and muscles.

I run around the *dojo* carrying my training partner on my back. It's hard work, but it's her turn next! A proper warm-up like this keeps us from straining our muscles.

We spend the morning doing *uchikomi*. We take it in turns to be attacker *(tori)* or defender *(uki)*. Getting an opponent off balance is the vital first step towards winning a fight. A good grip on the *judogi* helps to achieve this.

My opponent tries to throw me, but I am in a strong defensive position *(jigotai)*. She cannot unbalance me. If I used this position for long in a real match, I would be penalized for not attacking.

13

I pull on *uki's judogi* and sweep one leg from under her. This causes *uki* to lose her balance.

I have thrown *uki,* but without much strength or speed. A throw like this would not be good enough to score any points in a match.

I hook my leg around *uki's* and thrust against the top half of her body. This throw is called *ouchigari*. I use the weight of my own body to drive *uki's* shoulders down on to the mat.

This is a difficult throw called *uchimata*. I have thrown *uki* over my left hip. She has landed hard enough for me to score one half point *(waza-ari)*.

This throw is called *ukigoshi.* It needs quick footwork to trap *uki* and swing her over my right hip. She will hit the mat very hard. I would almost certainly score 1 point *(ippon)* for performing a throw as well as this in a match.

Judo matches can also be won by *osaekomi-waza*. This involves pinning *uki* to the mat for a certain length of time. She is trying to escape by using a bridge position to keep her body off the mat.

A fight can also be won by a stranglehold.
Once trapped in a hold, like this
okuri-eri-jime, uki can only pass out or else
submit by tapping *tori,* or the mat, with her hand.

It's my turn to be *uki* and I am about to submit! There is no escape from a powerful armlock, like this *jujigatame,* which can follow any throw, and would certainly end a fight by scoring *ippon.*

An actual fight lasts for only four minutes,
although it sometimes seems like four hours!

There is always more to learn in judo. My teacher *(sensei),* who has years of experience in top-level judo, watches me during my training sessions. We talk a lot about my performance and he coaches me.

I keep a judo diary. After each session, I write down what training I have done and how I feel about my performance. It is an important record of my progress and helps me to pinpoint areas for improvement.

On most evenings, I join in with the activities of my judo club. At the start of the session, the instructors line up in order of seniority opposite the pupils and everyone makes a respectful kneeling bow *(zarei).*

The members of the club do free practice
(randori) in pairs. I coach some of the
younger pupils.

There is no better way of learning the skills of judo than by practicing them. I teach older pupils by fighting with them. Here, my opponent is at the receiving end of a *tomoenage,* one of the most impressive throws in judo.

27

This is the scene at the Welsh National Championships. Several mats with red lines marking their edges are placed side by side. Two judges, a timekeeper, a recorder and a referee watch each match.

I beat all my opponents and so become the Welsh Ladies Champion at 123 pounds. It is a great honor, but I still have two years of hard work to do before I can achieve my dream of winning an Olympic medal.

Facts about judo

Judo is now practiced in over 100 countries. Over 400,000 Americans belong to judo clubs.

Judo became a modern Olympic sport in 1964.

The founder of modern judo was Professor Jigoro Kano who was born in Japan in 1860. He combined the best fighting styles from Japanese ju-jitsu training schools into the sport of Kodokan judo.

The word judo means "gentle way." Many skills in judo depend on giving way to an opponent's attack until the right moment to strike back This makes judo quite different from a sport like kendo (Japanese sword fighting) where the opponents attack each other with equal ferocity.

President Theodore Roosevelt was one of the first Americans to take up judo. He eventually became a brown belt.

The most successful *judoka* is Yashiro Yamashita of Japan. He won nine Japanese titles and four world titles in the 210 pounds weight group. He retired in 1985 undefeated after 203 successive wins.

The most successful woman *judoka* is Ingrid Berghmans of Belgium who has won six world titles.

There have been only seven 10th dan holders in the history of judo.

A judo match can be won outright by making one attack which scores one point *(ippon)* or by two attacks which score one half point each *(waza-ari)*.

GLOSSARY

Arm-lock
A hold which traps *uki's* arm.

Dan
A black belt *judoka*

Ippon
A match-winning throw or hold worth a score of one point.

Judoka (Jud-OH-ka)
A judo player.

Judogi (Jud-O-gee)
A judo suit.

Osaekomi-waza (O-say-kom-ee-WA-za)
Holding the opponent on the ground. *Tori* has to hold uke down for thirty seconds to score *ippon* or for twenty-five seconds to score *waza-ari*.

Randori (Ran-DOOR-ee)
Free practice.

Sensei (SENSE-eye)
A teacher.

Submit
To give up. The *judoka* who submits loses the contest.

Tori (Tory)
The attacking *judoka*.

Uchikomi (Oochee-KOWM-ee)
A series of repetitive exercises where a throw is practised again and again without actually throwing the opponent.

Uke (OO-kay)
The defending *judoka*.

INDEX

Arm-lock 2 8, 9, 21

Belt 3, 9
Bridge 19

Dan 9, 30, 31
Dojo 10, 11

Hold 2, 8, 9, 20, 31

Ippon 18, 21, 30, 31

Jigotai 13
Judo club 2, 3, 5, 25, 26, 30
Judogi 10, 12, 14, 31
Judoka 4, 8, 9, 30
Jujigatame 21
Ju-jitsu 30

Kano, Jigoro 30
Kendo 30

Okuri-eri-jime 20
Olympic Games 3, 30
Osaekomi-waza 19, 31
Ouchigari 16

Referee 28
Roosevelt, Theodore 30

Stranglehold 8, 9, 20
Submit 20, 21, 31

Throw 2, 8, 9, 13, 15, 16, 17,
    18, 21, 27, 31
Tomoenage 9, 27
Tori 12, 20, 31

Uchikomi 18
Uchimata 17
Uki 12, 14, 15, 16, 17, 18, 19,
    20, 21, 31
Ukigoshi 18

Waza-ari 17, 30